Little bub

Sid loved to sleep in Nat's doll's pram. He liked it when Nat tucked in the blanket and rocked him to sleep.

Nat and her pal Meg went on a trip with Sid in the pram. They met Miss Good on the street. Miss Good said, "I am off to the shops today to pick up my specs. They had to be fixed. I sat on them!"

Miss Good looked down at the pram.
She said, "Oh! You have a little bub! I do love them.
Let me have a look."

Nat said, "It is Sid, Miss Good."
"Oh!" said Miss Good.
"I like that. Good morning, little Sid."
Miss Good peeked into the pram.

9

"Let me pat his cheek. Little bubs have such soft skin."

Miss Good put her hand in to pat Sid.

"Well, he was born with a good lot of hair," she said.

At the shops, Miss Good
spotted Mum in the crowd.
She went up to Mum and
hugged her. She handed
her a gift bag.

Mum pulled out a bib! It said, "Mum's little bub" on it. Mum was shocked and said, "Thank you."

Miss Good burst out, "Oh, my dear! I have just met your sweet little bub. Such a cherub. Born with so much thick hair too!"

Mum was speechless.

Miss Good added, "Your
Sid is a darling bub!"

Words to blend

pram	blanket	went
spotted	trip	soft
skin	must	handed
gift	specs	peeked
morning	sweet	tucks
shops	darling	cherub
cannot	fixed	added

Before reading

Synopsis: Miss Good is going to collect her specs. When she encounters Nat and Meg with Sid in the pram, she calls him a little bub. Who does she think Sid is?

Review graphemes/phonemes: ee ow ur

Story discussion: Look at the cover and read the title together. Ask: *Who do you think this story is about? What might happen?*

Link to prior learning: Display a word with adjacent consonants from the story, e.g. *street*. Ask the children to put a dot under the single-letter graphemes (*s, t, r, t*) and a line under the digraph (*ee*). Model, if necessary, how to sound out and blend the sounds together to read the word. Repeat with another word from the story, e.g. *crowd*, and encourage the children to sound out and blend the word independently.

Vocabulary check: bub – an informal word for a baby

Decoding practice: Turn to page 9 and see how quickly children can find and read the word *sweet*. Can they find two other words with *ee* on the page too? *(peeked, sleeping)*

Tricky word practice: Display the word *love* and ask children to point out the tricky parts of the word (*o*, which makes the /u/ sound, and *ve*, which makes the /v/ sound). Practise writing and reading this word.

After reading

Apply learning: Ask: *How do you think Mum and Miss Good feel at the end of the story?* (Mum is really puzzled because Miss Good is calling Sid the cat a darling baby. Miss Good is feeling happy and congratulating Mum, because she thinks Mum has had a new baby.)

Comprehension

- How does Sid feel about sleeping in Nat's pram?

- Why does Miss Good think Sid is a baby?

- What gift does Miss Good give to Mum?

Fluency

- Pick a page that most of the group read quite easily. Ask them to reread it with pace and expression. Model how to do this if necessary.

- In pairs, have children read the conversation between Nat and Miss Good on pages 8–9, taking a part each.

- Practise reading the words on page 17.

Tricky words review

love	today	my
be	into	when
put	have	pulled
your	little	so
said	the	I